The Message

The extraordinary journey of an ordinary text message

Michael Emberley

A Caitlyn Dlouhy Book

ATHENEUM BOOKS FOR YOUNG READERS
New York London Toronto Sydney New Delhi

A message arrives.

Inside two little ears, microscopic hairs detect a disturbance in the air.

A brain thinks the sound is music.
Two eyes pivot toward the ringtone.

A pattern glows on a glass surface—
a message, radiating out as billions of
electromagnetic photons.

Special cells inside the eyes detect the photons, then translate the photon's message into an electric signal, which travels through soft threads of hollow nerves, filled with salty water, straight into the brain.

Electricity in the nerves of our bodies and brains is the same as electricity in copper wires, but it runs through salt particles rather than metal particles. We are electric creatures!

The signal leaps and hops across billions of microscopic synapses in the brain, leaving behind a salty electric trail.

Synapses are like street intersections for connecting nerves together.

**The signal's path draws an
electric map inside the brain.
The brain creates a thought from
that map and forms a response.**

*This signal map
in the brain is like
a computer chip,
processing and
storing information.*

This new message now begins an extraordinary journey, from this brain to another brain, thousands of miles away, on the other side of the world.

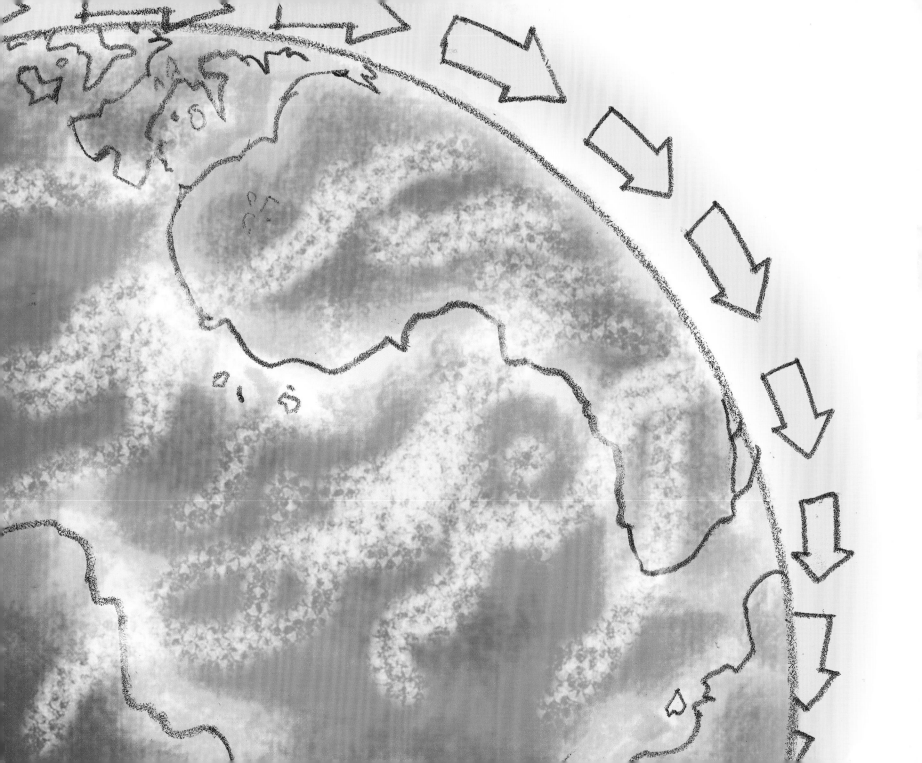

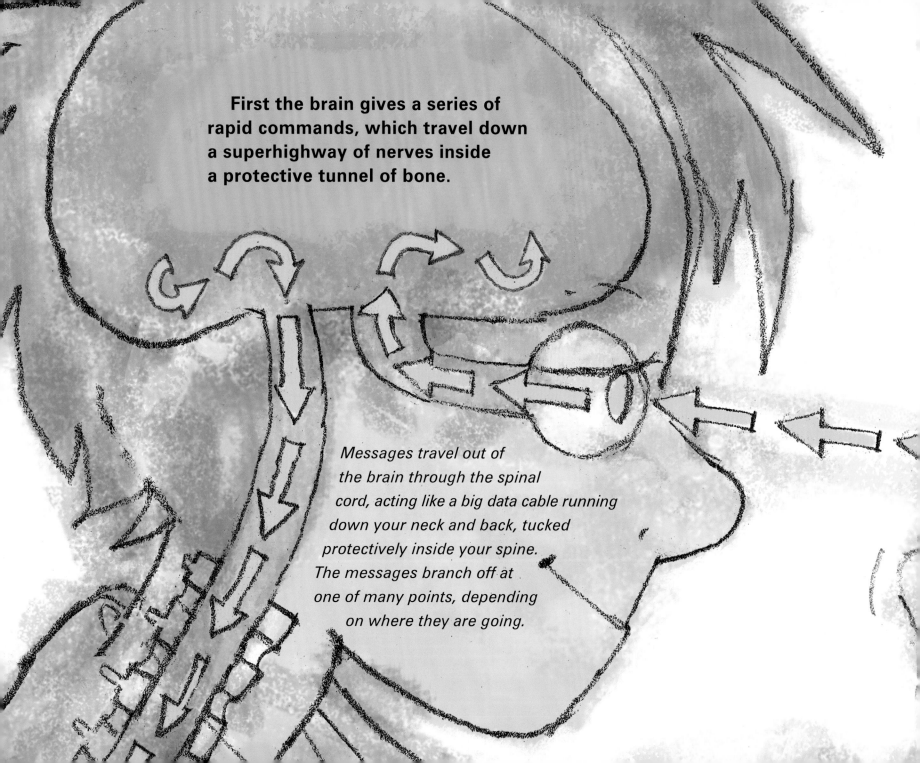

First the brain gives a series of rapid commands, which travel down a superhighway of nerves inside a protective tunnel of bone.

Messages travel out of the brain through the spinal cord, acting like a big data cable running down your neck and back, tucked protectively inside your spine. The messages branch off at one of many points, depending on where they are going.

Smaller nerves choreograph finger, muscle, and bone movement to flex and point. Nimble fingers perform a complicated tap dance over a set of symbols on a smartphone screen.

The brain has a part called the hypothalamus, which acts like a GPS compass, letting you know where your fingers are: up, down, left, or right. . . .

The smartphone senses a tiny electric charge inside each fingertip, letting it know where your fingers touch the screen.

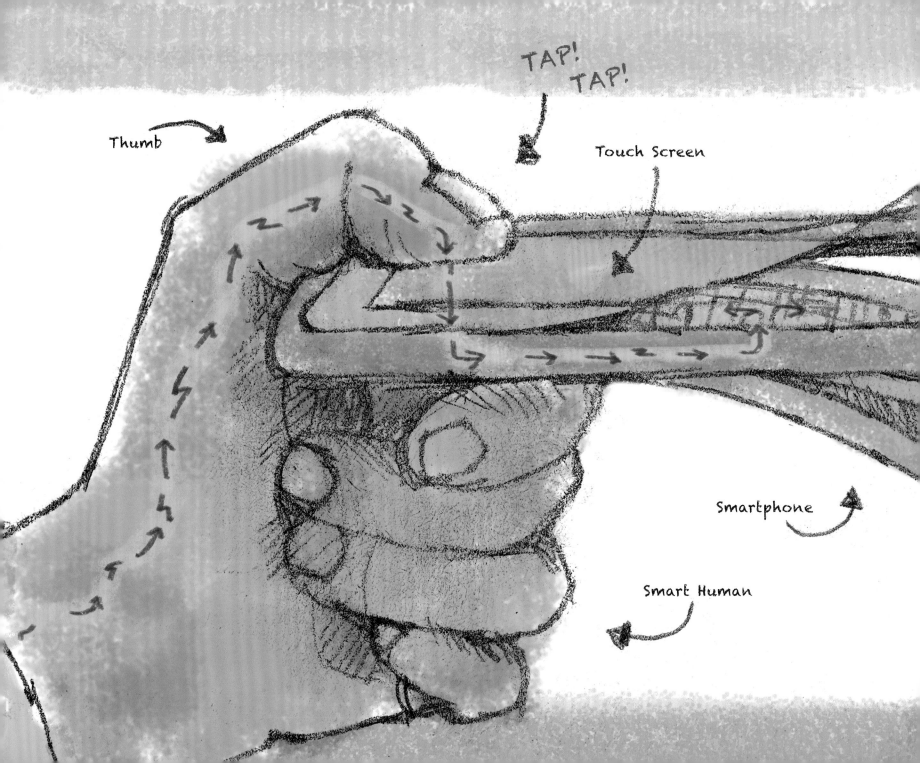

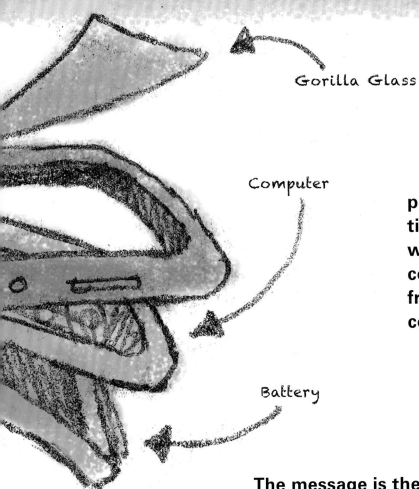

Gorilla Glass

Computer

Battery

Tiny electric charges inside fingertips pass through the glass screen, telling a tiny computer behind the glass exactly where the fingers are touching. The tiny computer translates the tapping pattern from human language into its own computer language.

The message is then beamed, in computer language, out of the phone and through the air. It doesn't aim for anything.

The message just . . . goes.

The message travels out through the air as a unique, invisible, electromagnetic radio wave . . .

. . . out through the huge electromagnetic field that surrounds the Earth.

All electromagnetic waves are the same thing, but different wavelengths—small, short waves or bigger, longer waves: radio waves, microwaves, gamma waves, X-rays, radar waves, infrared waves, ultra violet waves, even sunlight waves . . . all kinds of waves.

These rippling waves mix with and bounce off millions of other kinds of rippling waves.

You can't see them.
You can't feel them.
But they're always there.

Think of a magnetic field as a pond, and your finger as the message's radio wave: When you waggle your finger in the pond, it creates ripples. That's what a message does.

A spindly tower of bolts and steel
waits patiently, high on a hill, for
the ripple to reach it.

*Cell phone messages can go through
a thin wall, but not through big buildings,
mountains, or even bad weather. That's why
they are usually found somewhere high,
like the top of a hill.*

*There are about five million cell towers in the world. In the United States
alone, about sixteen million text messages are sent . . . per minute!*

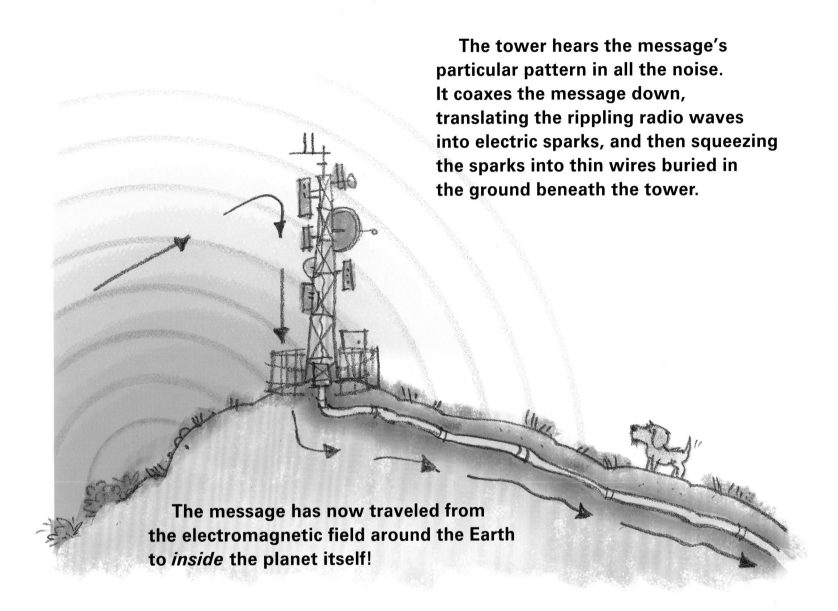

The tower hears the message's particular pattern in all the noise. It coaxes the message down, translating the rippling radio waves into electric sparks, and then squeezing the sparks into thin wires buried in the ground beneath the tower.

The message has now traveled from the electromagnetic field around the Earth to *inside* the planet itself!

Unless a text message is going a very short distance, it will travel much faster through a wire or fiber cable than through the air. But cell towers are important so you can walk around without being plugged into anything.

The message slips easily inside the wires.
It now speeds along underground, in the dark,
unseen by those above,

past worms and slugs, past bulbs and tree roots,
under beetles and rabbits, around caverns, sewers,
water pipes, and underground rivers . . .

. . . before arriving at an underground station
where the message is translated once again.
This time each electric signal is
transformed into pulses of light.

*Messages are whizzing past much more life below ground than
above it. The number of things living below ground—from animals
and plants to microscopic bacteria—is hundreds of times the
number living on the Earth's surface. (And twice the number
living underwater in all the oceans of the world!)*

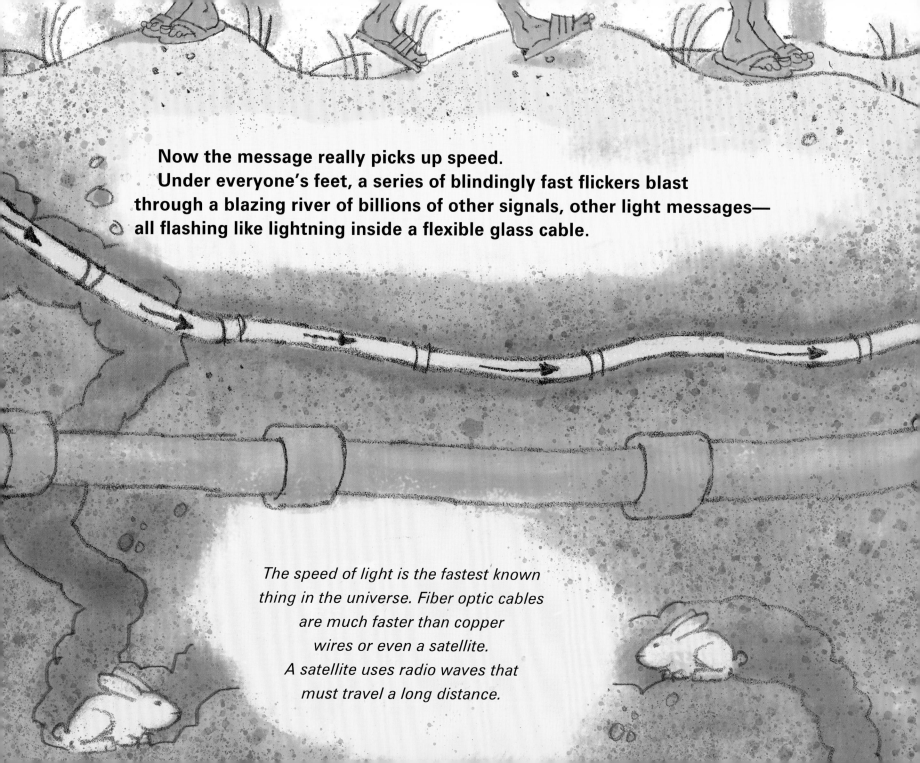

Now the message really picks up speed.
Under everyone's feet, a series of blindingly fast flickers blast through a blazing river of billions of other signals, other light messages—all flashing like lightning inside a flexible glass cable.

The speed of light is the fastest known thing in the universe. Fiber optic cables are much faster than copper wires or even a satellite. A satellite uses radio waves that must travel a long distance.

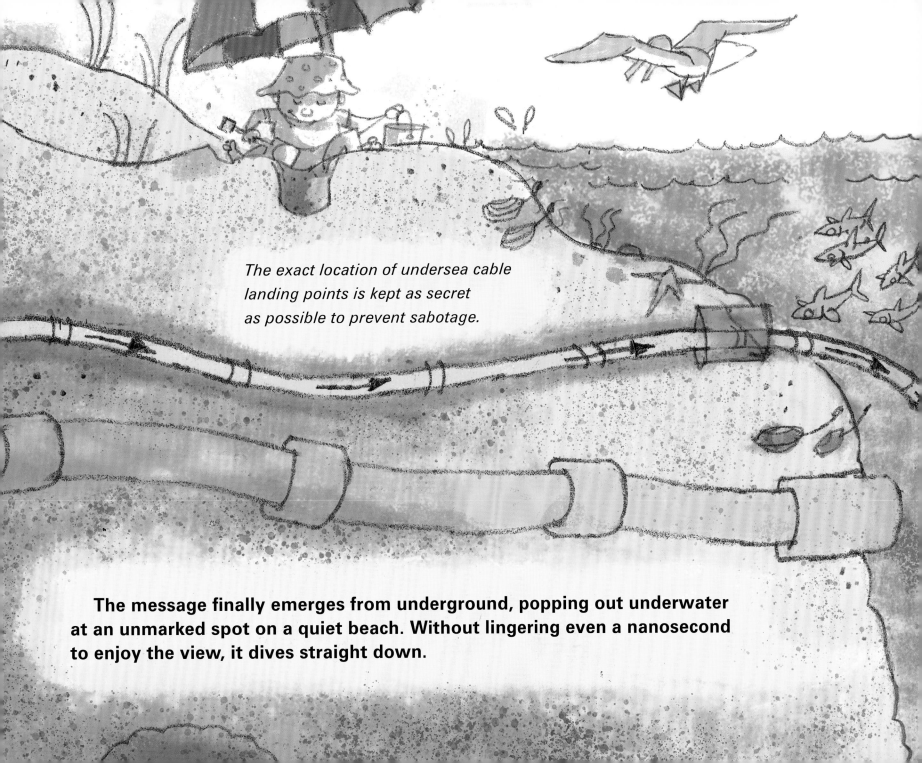

The exact location of undersea cable
landing points is kept as secret
as possible to prevent sabotage.

The message finally emerges from underground, popping out underwater
at an unmarked spot on a quiet beach. Without lingering even a nanosecond
to enjoy the view, it dives straight down.

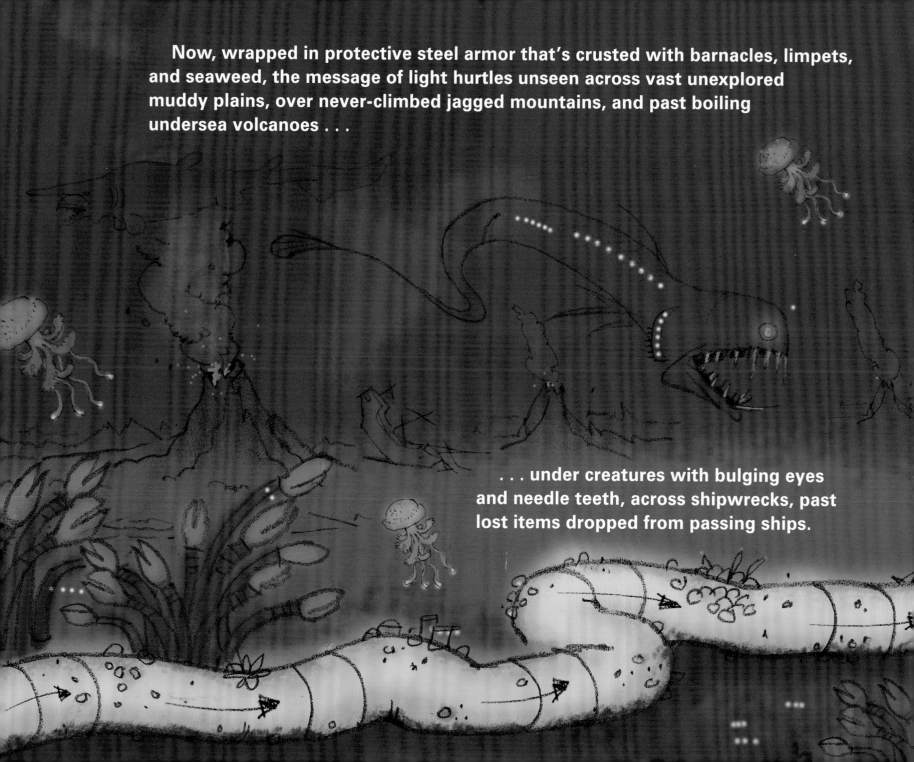

Now, wrapped in protective steel armor that's crusted with barnacles, limpets, and seaweed, the message of light hurtles unseen across vast unexplored muddy plains, over never-climbed jagged mountains, and past boiling undersea volcanoes . . .

. . . under creatures with bulging eyes and needle teeth, across shipwrecks, past lost items dropped from passing ships.

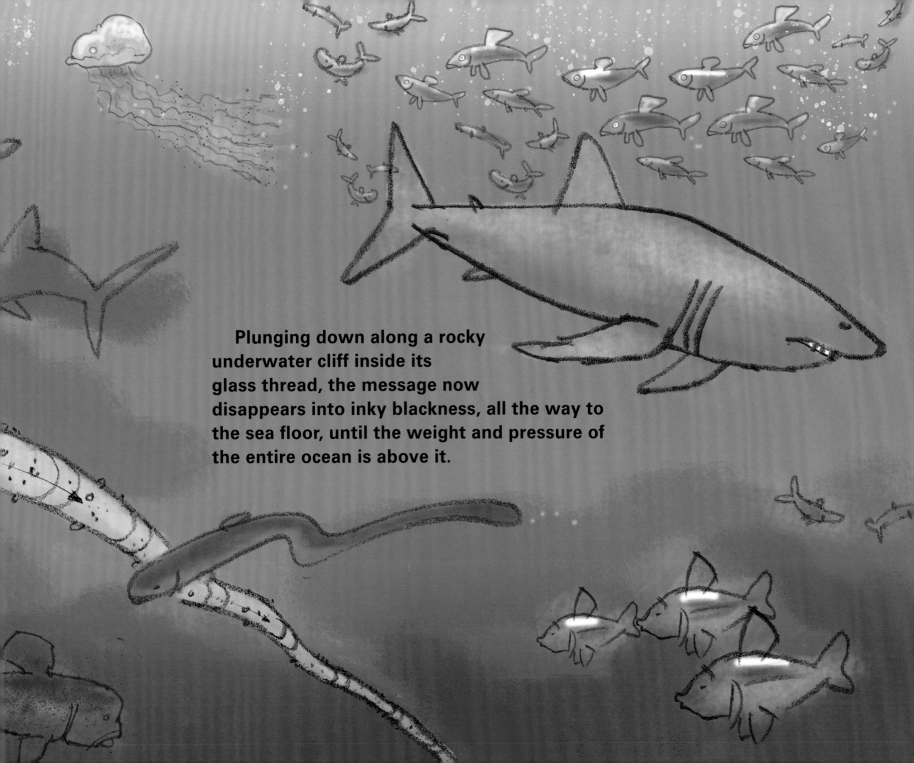

Plunging down along a rocky
underwater cliff inside its
glass thread, the message now
disappears into inky blackness, all the way to
the sea floor, until the weight and pressure of
the entire ocean is above it.

Only 10 percent of the ocean floor has been explored, so all messages sent across the sea pass through places no human has ever seen.

Cables are trailed out behind huge ships, like unwinding a giant ball of yarn, and left to sink thousands of feet down to the bottom of the sea.

At last the light message travels up, toward sunlight.
But without coming up for air, it burrows
back underground offshore, at a secret spot
hidden under another sandy beach.

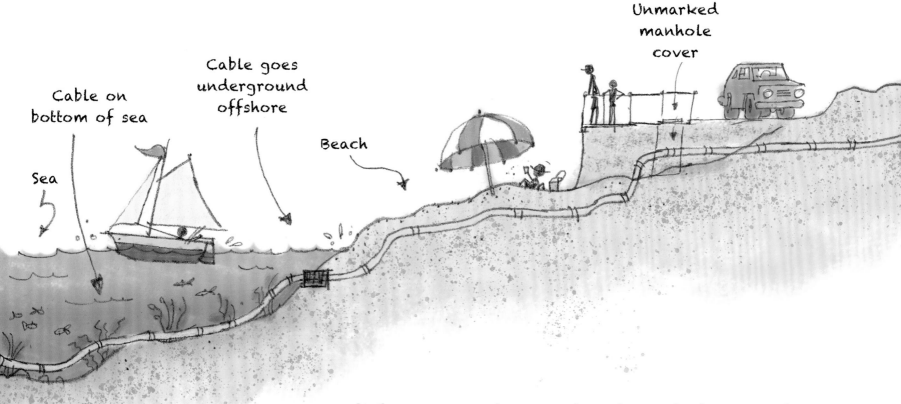

Unmarked manhole cover

Cable goes underground offshore

Cable on bottom of sea

Beach

Sea

It then races underground, under parked cars, under
streets and buildings, up another hill, to another waiting
tower—this one masquerading as a lonesome coastal pine.

From the top of this pretend tree, the message is broadcast out into the sky once again, rippling away as radio waves to yet another tower on top of an unmarked building.

Cell towers are sometimes made to look like local trees to blend in. In some places, such as Portland, Maine, they look like pine trees; in other places, such as San Diego, California, they look like palm trees.

Here, the message pauses in its journey—along with billions of other messages—to be sorted, stored, and shipped out, like post office letters, to addresses woven into the light flashes, mixed with all the messages shooting through the cable. The message has now been translated five times! From a thought in someone's brain, to electric nerve signals, to computer language, to radio waves, to an electric current, then to light flashes. And now it will be translated backwards—five times again—before reaching its final destination, in someone else's brain! Ten times the message is copied and rewritten—all in seconds!

Almost 2,300 working satellites orbit the Earth today. It's an outer-space traffic jam. Some provide your phone's GPS location for maps and rescue services.

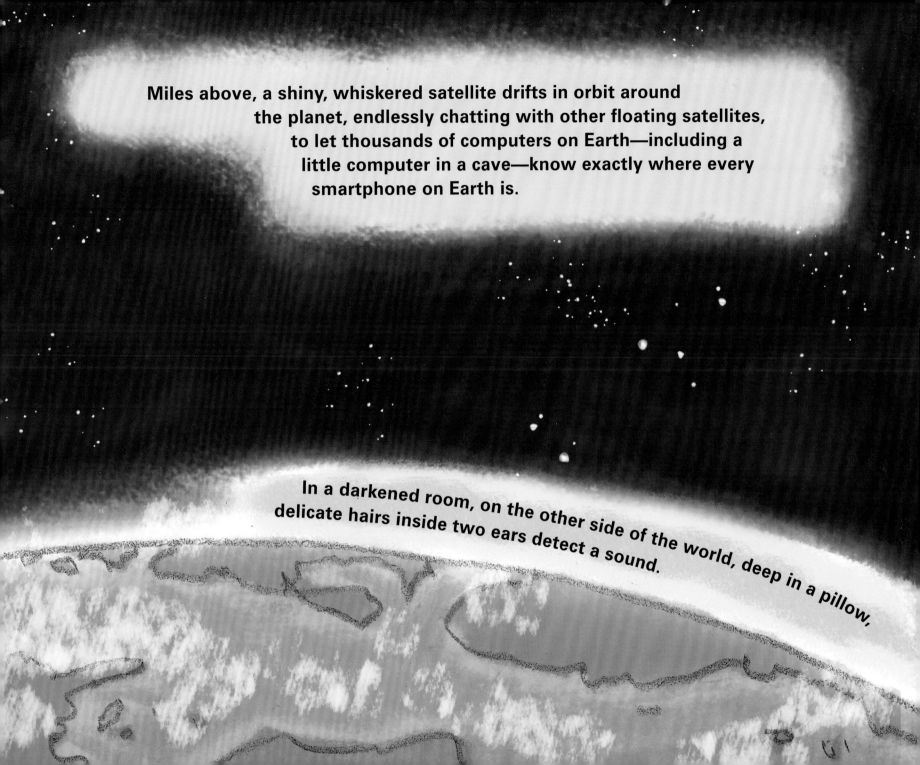

Miles above, a shiny, whiskered satellite drifts in orbit around the planet, endlessly chatting with other floating satellites, to let thousands of computers on Earth—including a little computer in a cave—know exactly where every smartphone on Earth is.

In a darkened room, on the other side of the world, deep in a pillow, delicate hairs inside two ears detect a sound.

The message has arrived.

The brain recognizes this particular jingling noise, directing its liquid electricity to power up eyes, hands, and fingers to make well-practiced movements to reach for a smartphone and open the message.

The message is instantly translated from computer language
back to human language in waves of light, where it's seen
by two sleepy eyes, passing the electric message along to a
half-awake brain.

Then, somewhere deep inside a fabric of a trillion
woven webs of chemical threads, a pattern emerges.

The message is decoded, and then greeted by a thought that begins jumping around the brain.

Then something else emerges from another part of the brain, a far more complex pattern than a simple thought.

An emotion stirs—

Emotions are far more complex than any text message or computer alone can generate. A text can, however, trigger an emotion to be created by the brain.

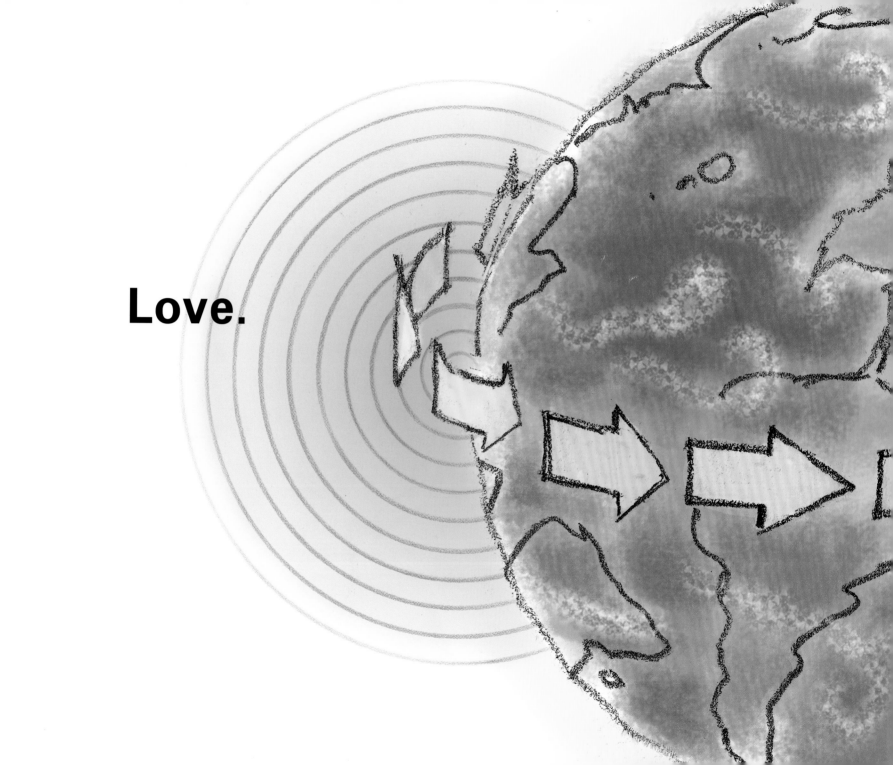

Love.

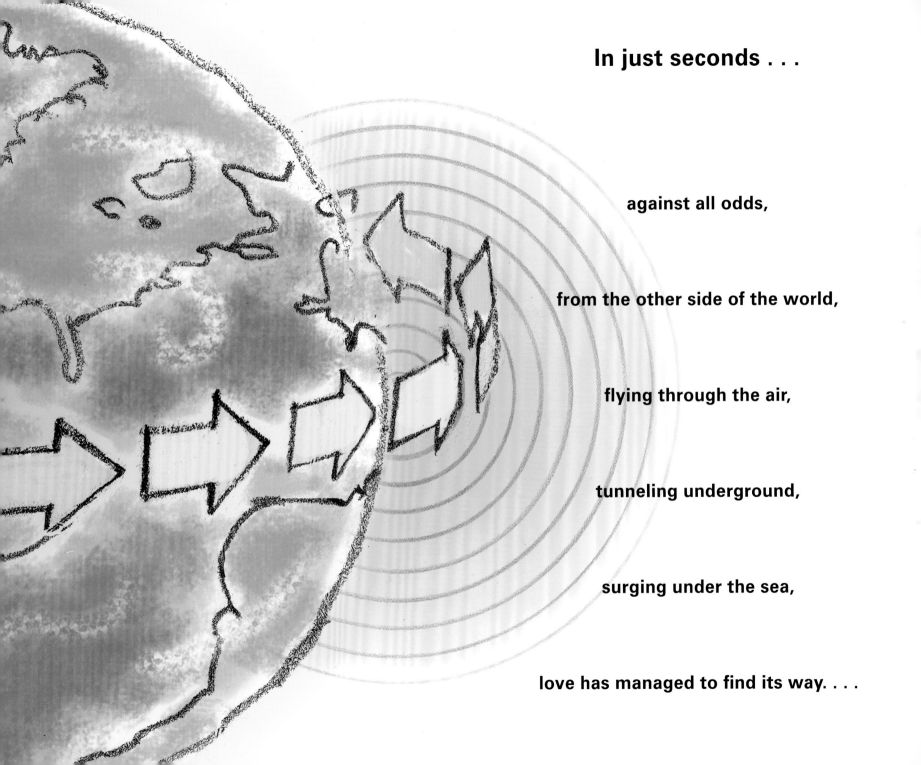

In just seconds . . .

against all odds,

from the other side of the world,

flying through the air,

tunneling underground,

surging under the sea,

love has managed to find its way. . . .

End of message . . .

until the next one!

SENDING A TEXT MESSAGE IS SO COMMON TODAY: sixteen million every minute in the United States. But rarely do we think about where our personal thoughts and feelings go after we hit send. Sending a text from, for example, Australia to Ireland takes only a few seconds, but the text doesn't instantly transport like magic; it still has to travel the whole way.

A cell phone has to have a tower in direct "sight" to work. A text message can go through a building, but not through a mountain. It leaves your phone as a radio wave signal, and then it's translated into an electrical signal to travel through an electrical wire, usually made of copper.

You can still send a message from almost anywhere in the world, including the middle of the ocean or a vast desert, but you'd need to pay extra for a special satellite phone and for the service. And it's expensive and slow. Having a conversation can be difficult because of the lag while the signal travels up into space and back. Plus, you need lots of satellites to make a connection. Again, like a regular cell phone, it has to have a direct line to the satellite.

A text message can race much faster through a wire cable than the air. That's why a regular text or call is sent through wires for most of its journey. It flies to the nearest radio tower, then down into wires, then pops up at the tower nearest to its destination, then flies to the person's phone your message was meant for.

A glass fiber wire cable is the fastest way of sending anything to the other side of the world. It translates the radio wave from your phone into a blinking light beam. And light can travel in a glass fiber as thin as a human hair, at the fastest speed anything can move in the universe—literally, "it makes the jump to light speed." Because it's so much faster, someday all copper wires may be replaced by glass fibers.

Because having wires strung all around the world, hung right above us like landline telephone wires, would be unacceptable, most of them are buried underground, or run along the bottom of all seven seas. There are thousands of buried cell phone cables and hundreds of hidden undersea cables cluttering up the ocean floor. And if you add the 2,300 or so working satellites floating above us, you can see that the convenience of instantly texting anyone we want in the world requires a massive infrastructure of mechanical and electrical equipment.

And that doesn't even begin to include all the equipment it takes to make the electricity to run all the power plants that send electricity to those innocent little wall sockets you plug your phone charger into. Some electric plants are run on nuclear power, some by oil-fueled generators. So you could say your phone runs on gas just like your car!

And finally, the websites you visit and applications you download, and even the whimsically named "cloud" computing, require actual wires and machines somewhere to function. "The cloud" just means your digital information, like texts and photos, is sitting on a large storage drive called a server, situated anywhere in the world, generally in a low-rent area, or even hidden in a cave. These servers don't hang out all on their own; there's usually a large building full of them sitting on long shelves like a public library. These buildings can burn down or flood just like any other building, so your online stuff is not living in a magic land safe from disaster. . . .